FOREST BOOKS

FAINT SHADOWS OF LOVE

KWANG-KYU KIM was born in Seoul in 1941 and studied German language and literature at Seoul National University. He later studied for two years in Munich. He first began to publish poems in 1975, the same year in which he published translations of poems by Heinrich Heine and Gunter Eich. In 1979 his first volume of poems was published, others followed in 1983, 1986, 1988 and 1990. Since 1980 he has been a professor in the German department of Hanyang University (Seoul) and he has published translations of 19th century German poems (1980), of poems by Bertolt Brecht (1985), of radio dramas by Eich (1986), and of poems by Eich (1987). He has been awarded a number of major Korean literary prizes for his poetry. The present volume is a translation of a selection from Kwang-kyu Kim's first three volumes of poems made by Professor Young-moo Kim (English Department, Seoul National University) and published with a critical introduction by him in Seoul in 1988.

BROTHER ANTHONY was born in Truro (Cornwall) in 1942. He has been a Brother in the Community of Taizé (France) since 1969. He went to Korea in 1980, and lives in Seoul with other members of the Community. He teaches English literature at Sogang University (Seoul). He is the translator of *Wastelands of Fire,* selected poems by Ku Sang (Forest Books 1990) and *A Korean Century*, River and Fields, also by Ku Sang (Forest Books 1991).

Faint Shadows of Love

Poems by
Kwang-kyu Kim

FOREST
BOOKS
London & Boston

Translated from the Korean
by Brother Anthony, of Taizé
Introduced by Young-moo Kim

PUBLISHED BY
FOREST BOOKS

20 Forest View, Chingford, London E4 7AY, U.K.
61 Lincoln Road, Wayland, MA 01778, USA

FIRST PUBLISHED 1991

Typeset in Great Britain by Cover to Cover, Cambridge
Printed in Great Britain by BPCC Wheatons Ltd, Exeter

Translations © Brother Anthony
Original poems © Kwang-kyu Kim
Cover illustration © Ann Evans

British Library Cataloguing in Publication Data
Kim, Kwang-Kyu
Faint shadows of love: poems
I. Title   II. Anthony, of Taizé, *Brother*
895.714

Library of Congress Catalogue Card No:
90–85574

ISBN 1 85610 000 6

Forest Books gratefully acknowledges the support of the
Korean Culture and Arts Foundation

Contents

Introduction

Kwang-kyu Kim has been heard to say that he normally writes his poems in the morning. Of course, he means quite literally that he usually physically writes before midday, but at the same time it may be possible to see there a metaphor for one of the major characteristics of his poetry; it seems to suggest that the clear-sighted, meticulous sensitivity of a freshly-wakened mind is one of the main qualities of his writing.

His are not poems inspired, for example, by extremes of enthusiasm or despair, hatred and enmity, with all the intoxication and rapture that implies; such poems may also spring from a mind that in a flash suddenly grows clear, after a torment of intoxication and hunger, despair and discouragement, excitement and passion. But Kwang-kyu Kim's poems are trimmed and polished in the morning light after a proper amount of sleep, and an adequate breakfast, they are the fruit of a calm and steady consciousness. The things and realities and people around, clearly seen and heard with firm self-control; those observations then precisely, logically, and systematically marshalled in simple words: such are the poems of Kwang-kyu Kim.

In words written for the cover of his first collection of poems (1979) he says 'one of the rights of life, a right that cannot be withheld, is to see and hear and think and speak reality as it is'. Therefore any attempt to withhold this right by manipulating, regimenting, or tempting a person's consciousness and desires is a sign of death, and this is closely linked for him with the feeling that life is not 'a pleasant state of anesthesia' but 'a waking pain'. Therefore the poem carefully written with morning's clear mind is, on the one hand, something designed to make clear the true character of the state of anesthesia in which the manipulated and regimented consciousness and desires are at home, and on the other hand invites self and reader to a pain that awakens from that state of unreal fantasy.

If then the process represented by Kwang-kyu Kim's poems is a passage from anesthesia to painful awakening, how should this be traced? A useful beginning would be among his very earliest poems, such as 'Spirit Mountain' (c. 1975). We may read this poem as a poem about the birth of a clear mind awakening from the falsehood of the world of ideals and dreams, all the yearning and nostalgia that we tend to experience in connection with childhood and home as well as anything essential and authentic. As we read this poem that arises so serenely with its 'I' carefully controlling feelings and betraying no emotions or thoughts, we are attentive to reflect in turn whether 'I' too do not somehow suffer from a similar painful loss of a childhood home and its mysterious mountain.

At the centre of the poem stands the mysterious mountain that is somehow there without being there, not visible yet glimpsed, not climbable yet present, and we are invited to perceive in the poem both the nature of the mountain and the mind which it continues to haunt. At one level there is a process of discovery; the spirit mountain is not located in space, it is no use taking a bus and going back to a place that is no longer there, for the mystery of the mountain has to be sought at other levels. The poem certainly does not report a simple loss of illusions; it does invite us to re-examine our evaluations of past experience.

In many of Kwang-kyu Kim's poems we find this theme of 'no return', often linked to the home and to childhood, but with something other than nostalgia. There is at the same time a feeling that the present has betrayed the past, that if the 'unfamiliar people' in the village deny the presence of the spirit mountain now, it is not that they are closer to the truth, but that they have fallen victim to the many forms of alienation present in contemporary society. The village home becomes the symbol of a polluted and shattered national identity.

Pollution and death are everywhere sensed and reported, so that this collection offers an impressive self-portrait of a society in which everyone is reduced, diminished to dwarfish and sub-human proportions. The dominant tone is not a sentimental regret for the past, but a dark satire of the dehumanizing results of those processes which the public authorities often term 'modernization'. As we leave our boring jobs and trail homewards we find ourselves compared to cold-blooded reptiles that in the evening return back to their swamp.

The group of readers that seems to be targeted in these poems is the urban 'middle class', especially the so-called *petit-bourgeois*, and we have to remember that in the early 1970s there was a controversy in Korean literary circles about the attitude that ought to be taken towards the mentality of this social sector. Simplifying the issues, the question was whether the mentality of the lower middle classes was something which should be defended or attacked. In more recent years the attention of many writers has been exclusively focussed on the 'Minjung', dramatizing in many ways the suffering of the workers, the poorest rural workers, the urban poor, in a populist spirit, marked by Marxism. As a result, the sufferings and plight of the lower middle classes have largely been ignored. Certainly there has been scant sympathy for them.

It is one of the achievements of Kwang-kyu Kim's poems that they have made many aware of the deeper roots of the frequently criticized attitudes of selfishness and compromise that seem at first sight to characterize the modern urban middle-class mentality. He explores in his poems topics that are more often the subject of novels and short stories than of lyric verse; here we find the selfish philistinism glimpsed in multiple moments of tiny gestures that strike home. The reason why he so meticulously examines the life of this one class is that he finds the mentality they exemplify equally present among workers, peasants and the urban poor. In the end, the 'general reader' is forced to admit that these portraits are only too familiar.

These carefully drawn portraits of our distorted selves, adults with dirty hands, display the superior talent of

Kwang-kyu Kim, to say nothing of the skills shown in the precisely drawn dense, compressed sketches of the basic patterns of the larger and more complex realities which produce such mental falsehood and paralysis. Together with the critical introspection of petit-bourgeois egoism and philistinism that is found in the novelistic details of certain poems, we find images of contemporary reality expressed in terms of allegorical symbols.

The basic characteristic of the suffocating Korean reality which we have experienced from the early 70s right through the 80s, and that he strives to communicate clearly to us in simple words, is a constant repetition of merciless violence. Everywhere we look we find images of a jungle full of a violence that knows no pity: conscience, ideology, exculpation, regret all equally set aside, the cicada is gobbled up by the spider, the long-prepared beautiful voice silenced in a flash by violence and fear. This reality is clearly expressed in many concrete and telling images. Even the cloudless autumn sky of which Koreans are traditionally so proud becomes a symbol and a source of nothing more than trembling anxiety. Purity can so easily be a mere absence of all the irregularities and variety that go to make up a truly human society.

The responsibilities are as clearly indicated as they can be; the baby crab that tries to return to the 'freedom of the sea' is mercilessly crushed by an army truck; there are references to a man who does not speak in words, who does not follow law, and who has no trace of humanity left in his dealings with others. 'I wonder who' has stifled all the normal activities of people in a happy free society; the riddle is quite transparent. Yet there is always the hope of resistance to the powers of silence and death; the miners trapped by a deadly underwater flood do not despair and hope is reborn with the passing of time. The cactus finally blooms after a long restless stay in the dark.

For it is life that triumphs here; the cancer cells within us too are welcomed as part of life, time is spent at night thinking of names for the unborn baby. The struggle against silence and death, the quest for freedom and hope only become more intense, not in a belief that there are always free spirits struggling in spite of oppression and darkness, but *because* of the surrounding darkness. Hope does not come after despair, but arises because despair presents itself as a possibility and is rejected. What we cannot reject or avoid is the fact of time, of ageing and final death; it is insofar as we recognize that our life's course is marked by that finality that we are enabled to create something utterly beautiful. Otherwise we fall asleep, back into the anesthesia. We cannot escape the fact that the lilac blooms on the rubbish dump, the lotus flower springs from the black slime.

When the poet tells the Korean bear that there is 'nothing new under the sun' he is not being worldly-wise and fastidious; he is telling the reader that the old is precisely the place of the new, if only you stop considering the past and look towards the future. The new comes springing from the old, but inevitably will in turn grow old, and in turn give rise to the new again, if people are not content to fall into the sleep of despair. Even death itself, so often for the Korean people a source of 'Han' (translated 'resentment'), is better understood as the fate of the seed out of which the new flowers spring.

For all these reasons we shall look in vain in Kwang-kyu Kim's poems for explosions of burning anger or fierce hatred in response to all the violence he so clearly sees. He does not consider anger and hatred to be proper responses to anger and hatred, although they may be quite natural and even healthy; in his work all is kept under control, violent gestures are steadily restrained. In the image of the pure autumn sky swept clear of every scrap of everything disagreeable by dictatorial radicalism, terrorism, and extremist activism, we may sense that the poet sees an identity of principles between those puritan attitudes and every kind of righteous anger.

Flattering themselves on their ownership of a free imagination, delicate and elegant, many self-styled 'elegant' poets in fact make use of such kinds of logic to shrewdly rationalize their own lack of practical concern. Thus Kwang-kyu Kim's approach here might be accused of being a form of self-justification for shunning the struggle to clear away the darkness invading social reality. But on closer examination, it can be seen that there is a vast difference between Kwang-kyu Kim's attitude and the basic approach of those poets who only abuse the freedom of the imagination, which has become a method, their sincerity a pose, in order to indulge in their own private hypnotic pleasures. After all, seeing righteous anger as boorish and avoiding it or rejecting it from the start, and controlling it are two quite different things, and Kwang-kyu Kim gives us an overall picture of the basic structures conditioning our reality, something that those poets cannot do. Kwang-kyu Kim invites us to set out along the ways of action with cool-headed precision.

Like the bad wisdom-tooth, he is not convinced that all the bad things in life can or should be simply and brutally uprooted. Uprooting means there is no hope of healing; but we are dealing with images for human life and the oppositions are not so simple. The flawless life and the distorted life are not a matter of either/-or, and the one cannot be opposed to the other so directly. Life may not be very possible in the daily life of present society, but running up into the unblemished nature of Kunak Mountain is not at all the solution, for nothing changes there. Nature and human existence follow different laws and values. In nature there are no conflicts of values, but mere being, followed by non-being, and that may be an envious state but in human reality what makes life truly cannot be found there. All that can happen is that the meaning of freedom and nature in human life may, indeed should, be gained by contact with those realities recognized among stones and animals and trees.

Thus the conclusion of these poems for modern humanity is that the extraction of the tooth and the flight into the hills are both false options, that it is within the present reality that another, dreamed-of reality of freedom and truth has to be constructed by choice and by struggle. And the unfrivolous normality of this vision, Kwang-kyu Kim's acute discernment as he eagerly examines with eye and ear the stuff of human lives, give us the adult quality of poems in which we encounter a morning mind quite free of all the fumes of anesthesia.

Young-moo Kim,
Professor, English Department,
Seoul National University.

Translator's Note

Major characteristics of Kwang-kyu Kim's poems are the simplicity of their language, and their wit. They are suggestive quests for hope in the midst of scenes of not-so-hopeful daily Korean life. Their greatest quality lies perhaps in their honesty, which is a word of high meaning in a world full of silence, hypocrisy and lies.

A short historical note may be useful for Western readers:

August 15, 1945, was National Liberation Day in Korea. For 36 years Korea had been ruled by Japan. The Japanese surrender at the end of the Second World War restored independence to the Korean Peninsula.

But the Cold War soon led to the horrors of the Korean War (1950–3) which ended with the division of the Peninsula by the 'Demilitarized Zone' along the 38th parallel that still separates North and South Korea in 1990.

When the first president of the Republic of Korea (South Korea), Syngman Rhee, tried to manipulate a 3rd term in office in 1960, the students of high-schools and universities took to the streets in peaceful protest demonstrations on April 19 of that year and many were brutally massacred.

Syngman Rhee fell, but then General Park Chung-hee took power in a military coup d'état in 1961, crushing all hope of democratic government. Under President Park the most dread social force was the notorious KCIA, a secret police force responsible for much repression, torture and violence.

After 1971, when President Park rewrote the Constitution ('Yushin') to make himself president for life, opposition and repression both grew. In October 1979 President Park was assassinated by the head of the KCIA, for reasons never made clear.

Again, the military imposed its will, and the rise of Chun Doo-Hwan culminated in a coup in May 1980, coinciding with the murderous repression of a popular struggle for democracy in the city of Kwangju. Again all opposition was violently repressed, speech controlled, the press gagged. Only the students continued to act as the nation's conscience.

April and May have special significance in Korea, linked as they are to the hopes frustrated in 1960 and 1980. The poems of Kwang-kyu Kim translated here were written under presidents Park and Chun, and they represent a courageous challenge to the officially-approved attitudes of submission and silence.

* * *

I would like to thank Professor Young-moo Kim for his enduring friendship. He and Professor Kwang-kyu Kim have both read my translations and they have helped me to avoid many foolish errors by their kind advice. The mistranslations which remain are no fault of either.

Brother Anthony, of Taizé

Spring 1975 —
Summer 1979

Ars Poetica

A dog stops suddenly
as it aimlessly wanders across an empty square
through the hard light of a summer noontide
and reaching its ears

from high on crowded concrete crosses
on vineyard slopes
sweetly unfolding out of light and water

a sound

left at the bottom of the sea while the fish
now corpses in the fish-market
stare up at us wordlessly
All those fishes' despairing names

not the borrowed names we use for a time
not a promise and unable to record
even the twittering of a sparrow
always stripped off thrown down crumpled

inadequate clothing of sounds . . .
language

although our mother tongues
clustered thick with consonants
are quite worn out before we can use them
someone who lives with language
fearless and unsorrowing
not looking for any blessing

but only pursuing sounds
that can never be spoken
treading in the footsteps of the wind
keeps repeating vain despair

Spirit Mountain

In my childhood village home there was a mysterious mountain. It was Spirit Mountain, and no one had ever climbed it. Spirit Mountain could not be seen in daytime. With thick mist shrouding its lower half and clouds that covered what rose above, we could only guess dimly where it lay. By night too Spirit Mountain could not be seen clearly. In the moonlight and starlight of bright cloudless nights its dark form might be glimpsed but yet it was impossible to tell its shape or its height.

One day seized with a sudden longing to see Spirit Mountain – it had never left my heart – I took an express bus back to my home village but strange to say Spirit Mountain had utterly vanished and the now unfamiliar village folk I questioned swore that there was no such mountain in those parts.

Being and non-being (I)

The red brick building of the dye store
soaked by springtime rainfall
takes on a strange tint you'd not find in a colour-chart

That tint that no one takes note of
lingers briefly on roof and walls
then slips away from the house again

A sharp-eyed pigeon flies
up into the haze where chimes echo
up after that tint as after something
that might be seen and caught

At last the flying pigeon returns exhausted
perches on the TV antenna of the house next door and
stares down vacantly at the brick building stained with dye

Being and non-being (II)

It vaguely wandered far off just above the horizon, and it spun around me too, very close by.

Fluttering like a butterfly it settled on my shoulder, scurrying away like a squirrel when I stealthily reached up a hand, then when I ran panting after it, it suddenly penetrated into my body constricting my breast.

Once I clung hold of something that had come close beside me. Something cold-blooded and slithery like a snake writhed trying to escape from my hand. Like in a wrestling match we grappled this way and that but finally it got away. For it had no trunk or head or limbs or wings and could not be seen.

It kept following me and all the time I kept pursuing it.

Sometimes I came across it in a bookstore but on inspection it would turn out to be just a book. Occasionally I glimpsed it in the market or in a store but what I seized would turn out to be a fish or a fruit or a suit or such like. Once I saw it walking along in the shape of a smartly-dressed middle-aged man and followed him but he was just a run-of-the-mill insurance-office clerk. I hastened to examine a place brightly lit up at night but it was only a petro-chemical complex operating non-stop.

At last I discovered it in a hitherto unknown alley-way I had entered by chance. It was the back of a seedy house I felt I had often seen somewhere before. It was a messy scene to one side of a half-sunlit storage terrace with worn-out pieces of furniture strewn around and a chimney standing askew in one corner.

Emerging from that alley-way I was surprised to see it among passers-by and cars and trees and cigarette-kiosks and roadside pushcarts. It seemed to be visible everywhere in the world.

But when I tried to grasp it it was nowhere to be found.

I

Come to think of it
I am
my father's son
my son's father
my older brother's younger brother
my younger brother's older brother
my wife's husband
my sister's brother
my uncle's nephew
my nephew's uncle
my teacher's pupil
my pupil's teacher
my country's tax-payer
my village's army-reservist
my friend's friend
my enemy's enemy
my doctor's patient
my regular bar's customer
my dog's master
my household's family head

therefore
I am a
son
father
younger brother
older brother
husband
brother
nephew
uncle
pupil
teacher
tax-payer
army reservist
friend

6

enemy
patient
customer
master
family head
not just
one I

tell me then
what is that I
that no one knows
and this I
standing here now
who am I?

Future

Arrival Seoul 19:30
just as it's written in the timetable
Carrying dolls with fancy labels
the first-class train rushes by and then
empty tracks remain in the early summer plain

A little school-girl goes plodding
along zig-zag paths over banks and dykes
the breeze stroking
her white blouse and black skirt
How completely unthinkable her life ahead
Reflected in the water of the paddy-fields
it dazzles my eyes

Summer's day

I want to run
I want to go rolling
down steep mountain slopes
overgrown with brambles
pouring blood
like a guerilla
hit by machine-gun fire
I want to moisten my tongue
in the dew on the grass
become a bird and fly
deep into the mountain gorges

I want to go tumbling
I want to pour out
my last drop of sweat
kneeling under the midday sun
on a shore ever battered by rolling waves
yet never reduced
I want to sink
naked like a stone
into deep underwater ravines
leaving my shadow behind
I want to go back
I want to wander
breathing moist darkness
having gone back into the forest
where sultry sap surges
and having lost my way
I want to totter
sink down
and flow into the ground

A patriot's biography

In the government offices they called him a Special Case.

From early childhood he cared for heretics fallen in the streets, as a youth he protected cunning and brutal criminals and as soon as he was old enough he frequented seditious groups and entered the underground movement.

The times were always turbulent.

There was absolutely no way he could sleep quietly, eat with pleasure, earn money and live happily, and therefore he believed that doing such things was wrong.

Ever preferring heart to body, he was someone who pursued a great and lofty goal, as numerous anecdotes testify.

And before mounting the scaffold he, who could never be calm like a sage, requested a cigarette and a glass of wine.

I don't know if his last wish was granted.

But when the moment came for him to be separated from his body, instead of shouting out defiance boldy, he became a weak human being and trembled.

You know, what touches me most is his end, when he could not act like a patriot.

Requiem

Perhaps he never existed to begin with?
So I reflected as I stood beside the sea
at the crack of dawn watching an hour-glass
and sometimes as I paused before a red light
at a level-crossing
No
He definitely existed
He left behind
his clothes hanging beside the window
waving in the breeze
his glasses laid askew on the desk
five stubbed-out fag-ends
as well as half a bottle of his favourite liquour
Perhaps he's just gone away?
Casting off expression voice and gesture
and finally even his body
Perhaps it's us who are left behind
after seeing him off?
No
Leaving his shoes at the door
he has suddenly gone inside
Vanished inside memory
Then perhaps we are outside?
Perhaps we are lingering outside
looking for him?
No need for that
Nothing can conceal him now
or hide us
He exists in most vivid form
inside
Don't think of him
Look at him

Epitaph

He never read a line of poetry
not one single novel
he lived happily all his life
he earned a lot of money
rose to high position
and left this magnificent tombstone
And some famous literary figure
wrote here an epitaph eulogizing him
Even if the world is reduced to ashes
this stone will firmly resist the heat
of the flames and survive
to become a precious historical document
Then what the hell does history record?
What tombs will poets leave?

Home

Fish with crooked backs
live in the River Han
Baby fish with crooked backs are born
and though they pant and gasp
they cannot leave Seoul's sewer
They do not head sea-wards
A place you cannot leave
and now a place you can't return to
Is such a place a home?

Spring song

As the snow melts
the hills and fields
are plunged deep in thought

While the plain gropes after vague memories
its weeds have regained their proper height
On the poplar trees with their good memories
in just the same spot on each branch
buds are meticulously bursting

Azaleas recall days gone by
and blush
in mountain valleys drifts a scent of rutting
the streams pour down fresh passion
women on the pill give birth to sweet
children of death

After a while waking from their thoughts
mountains and fields gradually grow
and men build new appartment blocks
becoming that much more estranged from home

Going home in the evening

We gave up any thought of flying long ago

These days we don't even try to run
we dislike walking so we try to ride
(we mostly travel about by bus or subway)
Once on board we all try to get a seat
Once seated we lean back snoozing
Not that we are tired
but every time money-making is over
our heads become atrophied
scales sprout all over our bodies
Our blood has grown cold
but still with half-open eyes
our practised feet take us home

We return every evening to our homes
like reptiles going back to their swamp

The voice of water

Between the hills and fields and trees and sky
that sway like seaweed
look what can be seen on the boundless earth

Birds fly flapping pitiful wings
animals trot awkward on four legs
cars roll on wheels
planes are borne on the wind
people walk precariously on two feet

They brew and drink endless thirst as wine
make gods in imitation of water
then unearthing oil revolt against water
by day flesh moves and smiles as face
by night in twos they play their clumsy games
and once again wash dirty bodies in water

Abandoned tribes of metal
kindling fires of parched time
spitting on rotting fingertips and counting money
in that way may you be a whole lifetime dissatisifed
may you suffer many more deaths
The blessings of water are not bestowed

Ducks

Holy bird!
Never ever perching
in branches of trees of comfort
those trees that grow straightest
if not completely vertical
that generate no electricity
A duck is not one for lying down or getting up
Quietly wandering over winter river water
it merely repeats simple gestures
It has not picked up any complicated habits
Sometimes it leaves water prints
in the snow-covered ice
and if an earthquake comes
riding the whirlwind it flies up
up into the sky
casting a final shadow
destined to become a fossil
on the land of death
Most perfect bird!
The place from which the duck comes flying
and to which it returns
is a place I have come too far from
Borne on trains traversing continents
crossing oceans by aeroplane
I have travelled so far in any case
that now it is impossible for me
to cross that far horizon and return
How happy is the duck returning
with unthinking wing-beats
whenever the seasons change
If I am ever to return to that place
I must first forget with groans of pain
all the language I have so arduously learned
With far greater difficulty than in the gaining
I must lose one by one all the things I know
Useless the pitiful body's writhing

as it tries to rise and rise again
then lie down and lie down again
At last I shall have to set out alone
How envious then is the life of the duck
that flies and flies then drops plop dead
Blessed bird
serenely frequenting that far-off place
I can never return to so long as I live
There are times when I long to be a duck

Today

When the sound of chimes rings out from the church
I get up and throw open the window
then draw in deep refreshing breaths
That sweet odour of lead from exhaust fumes
floating through the early morning air!
Health is truly a grace of God
As I duly eat my morning rice
mixed with mercury-bleached bean-sprout soup
then ride to work on a crowded bus
I always love today especially
Today is the day to pay the month's instalment
to the building and loans society

At nine o'clock I stand
before a daily growing metal mass
feeling the prickly glare of instruments
Suddenly emerging from the metal a cricket's chirp
a frog's croak
this metal so utterly incapable of error
sometimes makes me feel sinful
How can I be asked to be sorry
for forty years lived according to safety first?
I must pray saying I repent

With thick glasses over bloodshot eyes
today as usual I rummage in litter bins
searching among fag-ends and messy doodles
and inside crushed soft-drinks cans
for conspiracies hidden there
All day long I carefully rummage in litter bins
and if I cannot find anything
my heart grows more anxious still for
who could believe in a world without conspiracy?

An annual interest of 10% maturing in 15 years
I spend the day absorbed in calculating costs

19

and in the evening I meet my friends
Smart fellows together
winners and losers versus today
drinking so as not to get drunk
making uproar so as not to talk
driven out by the midnight curfew
making our way home
bringing up what we have eaten
beside an alley-way telegraph pole
weeping a moment tears clear as rice wine
we gaze up at the hazily shining stars

In this treeless village once TV is finished
we each and all give the house over to the dogs
and snoring virile snores sleep others' sleep
— it's even OK to look angry
You bastards just you show your faces quick
— it's even OK to swear
You bastards just you speak up quick
and just you think for once
who do you think's the boss here?
But every time we wake up
we forget
all the things we hear in dreams
though the ear gets used to hearing them there

While eating a flounder

From the earliest days we've always believed
that we were like God
or that God resembled us

With an eye and an ear and an arm and a leg
to left and to right to right and to left
of a mouth eager to speak and genitals eager to be hid
we have always compared right with left
made balances and wheels and raised up walls

Unable to bear what was not divided
we divided the freely scattered hills fields and sea
between right and left

and in just the same form as our bodies
we made dolls and medals and weapons
while in imitation of our heads
we erected churches offices and schools

Finally we divided even sounds and light and stars
between right and left

and we cannot now help dividing our heads and bodies
so we choose to drink as we eat raw fish
While the flounder trembles and flutters
at the strangeness of our shapes
we tear at its body and eat it alive
only laughing to observe how both its eyes
are oddly fixed on the right-hand side

but even now we don't realize
This flounder simply cannot be divided
into right and left left and right
and we do not realize
what it might possibly resemble

Faint shadows of love

At the end of the year of the April Uprising
we met at five in the afternoon
happily clasped hands in greeting
then sitting in a chill fireless room
our breaths condensing white
we engaged in heated discussion
Foolishly enough we believed
we were living for the sake of something
for something that had nothing to do with politics
The meeting ended inconclusively and that evening
drinking grog at Hyehwadong Rotary
we worried in a pure-minded way
about problems of love and spare-time jobs
and military service
and each of us sang as loud as he could
songs no one listened to
songs no one could imitate
Those songs we sang for no reward
rose up into the winter sky
and fell as shooting stars

Eighteen years later at last we met again
all wearing neckties
each of us had become something
We had become the older generation
living in dread of revolution
We chipped in to cover the cost of the party
exchanged news of our families
and asked the others how much they were earning
Anxious about the soaring cost of living
happily deploring the state of the world
expertly lowering our voices
as we discussed rumours
We were all of us living for the sake of living
This time no one sang
Leaving abundant drink and side-dishes behind us

noting one another's new phone numbers we parted
A few went off to play poker
A few went off to dance
A few of us walked sadly
along the university street we used to frequent
Clutching rolled-up calendars under our arms
in a place returned to after long wanderings
in that place where our love gone by had bled
unfamiliar buildings had appeared suspiciously
the roadside plane trees stood in their old places
and a few remaining dry leaves trembled
sending shudders up our spines
Aren't you ashamed?
Aren't you ashamed?
As the wind's whisper flowed about our ears
we deliberately made middle-aged talk about our health
and took one step deeper into the swamp

The land of mists

In the land of mists
always shrouded in mist
nothing ever happens
And if something happens
nothing can be seen
because of the mist
for if you live in mist
you get accustomed to mist
so you don't try to see
Therefore in the land of mists
you should not try to see
you have to hear things
for if you don't hear you can't live
so ears keep on growing
People like rabbits
with ears of white mist
live in the land of mists

A ghost

Hush!

Look at that black car
speeding through the dark
Look at those men in everyday clothes
vanishing up side-streets smoking cigarettes
Look at those oil marks
spreading over the devastated earth
look at those pieces of iron
littering every roadside

if you cannot see the shape of the ghost
you must all be blind!

Within the flying dust and cement
that enter our lungs each time we breathe
until at last it seems we must suffocate

if you cannot hear the voice of the ghost
you must all be deaf!

Hear the voice of those corpses
rotting sunk in some deep pond
Hear the voice of those breaking bodies
that rise smoking from every chimney and fill the sky
Hear the groans that to the bitter end
do not emerge from mouths clenched tightly shut
Hear those shouted commands that rise
from a treeless sandy plain

Hush!

Conversation drill

(In the land of mists I wanted to make friends with many people. I also wanted to bargain for low prices when I was buying things. But my words failed completely to get across. The reason was my ignorance of the following basic conversation pattern.)

No
That's wrong
I disagree

Yes Sir
That's right Sir
I agree Sir

Of course
You must always agree
It is not possible to disagree with me
In your dictionary the word disagree does not exist
and in my dictionary the word agree does not exist

So we use the same words
but our dictionaries are different Sir
I will be more careful in future Sir
and before you disagree I will agree

Between ideas

Now if
a poet thinks of nothing but poems
a politician thinks of nothing but politics
a businessman thinks of nothing but business
a worker thinks of nothing but labour
a judge thinks of nothing but law
a soldier thinks of nothing but war
an engineer thinks of nothing but factories
a farmer thinks of nothing but farming
a civil servant thinks of nothing but administration
a scholar thinks of nothing but study

it may seem that the world will become a paradise
but in actual fact

if there is no one thinking of the relation

between poems and politics
between politics and business
between business and labour
between labour and the law
between the law and war
between war and factories
between factories and farming
between farming and administration
between administration and study

then nothing but
scrap paper and
power and
money and
exploitation and
prisons and
ruins and
pollution and
pesticides and
repression and
statistics

will remain

Almanac

When spring comes they will awake
Stretching they will try to rise
Prevent them from rising
Teach them how sweet
is a morning bed

Tidy those hills up neatly
where rocks lie scattered in disorder
plant only trees that can be used for lumber
and make them grow straight

Make them happy with the early summer breezes
that bring flowery balm to every scratch that
the branches make as they pass through acacia groves

Make them thirsty
by the burning sun of June's month-long drought
submerge them in water
by the pouring rains of July's month-long monsoon

Make the curving meandering rivers
flow in straight lines
and to the child born there in the apartment block
just above the embankment
instead of a name give a number

Frighten them by banks of late-autumn mist
that cover the mountain peaks
and drop down through the pine groves behind the villages

When winter comes they will feel cold
Shivering they'll try to draw near the fire
Prevent them from drawing near
Tell them that when winter goes the spring will come
Make them hibernate

Small men

They are getting smaller
They keep getting smaller
Before they'd finished growing
   already they'd begun to get smaller
Before they first fell in love thinking about war
   they began to get smaller
The older they get the smaller they get
As they break off a yawn they get smaller
As they shudder from terrifying nightmares
   they get smaller
Jumping every time someone knocks they get smaller
Hesitating even at a green light they get smaller
As they lament that they don't grow old quick enough
   they get smaller
As they bury their heads in the newspaper
   the world is so calm they get smaller
Standing neatly in line wearing ties they get smaller
As they all think about earning money doing business
   they get smaller
As they listen to inaudible orders they get smaller
As they repeat words identical as uniforms they get smaller
As they fight with invisible enemies they get smaller
As they attend multiple meetings and clap they get smaller
As they consume luncheons of power and pick their teeth
   they get smaller
As they grow fat and play golf they get smaller
As they go to cocktail parties and drink scotch
   they get smaller
As they embrace their wives now grown too stout
   they get smaller

They have grown small
At last they have grown small
They have grown smaller than the quick-eyed sparrows
   that fly up to the eaves from the garden
Now they know how to smoke while wearing a mask

They know how to laugh louder than ever at unfunny moments
They know how to be sincerely sad for long periods
    about things that are not sad
They know how to keep happiness hidden deep down
They know how to evaluate correctly each kind of anger
They know how not to say what they really feel
    and to cast furious glances at one another
They know how not to think of questions nobody asks
They know how to count their blessings
    every time they pass a prison
They all know how to take an umbrella and walk down
    alley-ways when it rains
Instead of dancing in the plains
    they know how to sing falsetto in bars
When they make love they know how to cut back on
    uneconomical wearisome caresses

Truly
they have grown small
They have grown quite small enough
all that is left is their Name Occupation and Age
now they have grown so small they are invisible

so they can't get any smaller

Death of a baby crab

One baby crab
having been caught with its mother

tumbles out of the hawker's basket
while the big crabs fixed in a straw rope
foam and wave aimless legs
and crawls off sideways sideways over the roadway
in quest of past days of hide-and-seek in the mud
and the freedom of the sea
It pricks up its eyes and gazes all around
then dies squashed across the roadway
run over by a speeding army truck

Where the baby crab's remains rot in the dust
no one sees how the light of glory shines

A journey to Seoul

As you pass Pyongtaek on the way up to Seoul
crossing the evening plains full of autumn smoke
perhaps in the shaking window you
may glimpse your suddenly unfamiliar face
Do not think that is yourself!
Are there not familiar faces beside you
gnawing dried squid and playing cards?
As you look at the screaming bright roofs
in the twilight and the TV antennas
fluttering like dragon-flies
and your fascinating weekly magazine
nod your head!
Do not listen to painful sounds
like the calling of grasshoppers
poisoned by pesticides
like the radio hiss
when the late-night programmes are over!
Aren't the energetic songs
played from every roadside loudspeaker cheerful?
And the sound of cars speeding along the motorways?
People have long compared life to a journey
As you drink your beer or cola
have a pleasant journey!
Don't think at all!
When you are surprised
just say Ah!
If you want to say more keep quiet!
When silence feels awkward
talk about the long drought
about the Argentina football match
about the rising GNP and the stock market!
For your own sake
and for mine

A small stockholder's prayer

Almighty God!

As you may already know a high building recently collapsed.

Nobody imagined that such a solid steel-and-cement 79-storey building would suddenly fall down like that. And I was no exception. Although I didn't know which big corporation it belonged to but only gazed from my distant house at that building soaring up in the city-centre, my heart used to feel safer because we had such a national resource and I used to think how one day when funds permitted I too would go up to the sky-lounge on top and drink at least an orange juice. But then one day that high building suddenly fell down.

Moreover as that building fell in the direction of my house the 3000 ton cooling tower standing on its roof flew off and landed on my home, robbing me in a flash of my family and fortune. It is so astonishing I've had no time to be sad. I simply cannot make any sense of this incredible situation.

As you know I am a law-abiding citizen and have always been a model head of my household.

As you will see if you consult my curriculum vitae and my personal record files, I have until now never failed to observe even one of the laws and usages of society. Since childhood I have honoured my parents, respected my teachers, done my national service, loved my family, always paid my taxes in due time, been a sincere believer, I put by savings when I could, and prayed in a special way that they might strike oil in our country too. I don't smoke, I don't drink, I don't go with women, and nowadays I've even stopped drinking coffee. Of course I haven't been able to contribute huge amounts to the National Defence Fund, but still when I use the pedestrian overpass I never go by without tossing a coin to the beggar kneeling on the steps.

And yet there can be no doubt that in suddenly loosing family and fortune I am receiving divine punishment. But I cannot find out what earthly sin I can have committed to deserve this.

God, give me back my reason and give me strength to think correctly. Make me able to grieve properly for my lost family and fortune. And give me enduring faith in that future they promise us here, a paradise.

Amen.

Delayed enlightenment

By chance we were born brothers
My elder brother
loved to play at soldiers
and he became a general
all covered in medals
I used to love to paint
I became a private
painting cobblestones
Maybe life's like that at times
but soon it's got to change
Counting the days to discharge
that's how I used to think
Our older sister
born to keep us company
bright as a doll
became the wife
of a well-to-do company chairman
I used to like to cry
I became a worker wearing glasses
Life is really an unknowable thing
but at least everyone goes his own way
As I waited for the bus that didn't come
that's how I used to think
We were all born fellow-countrymen
Some have become administrators ruling us
or wage-earners faithful like dogs
or housewives taking fish home
others have been put into prisons
built by their own hands
History always changes and
is always the same
always on the side of the winners
but there are always more on the losing side
There's no way you can start all over again
but you can't let it end like this
That's how I think now

Autumn 1979 –
Summer 1983

An old old question

Who doesn't know that?
As time flows on
flowers wither
leaves fall
and one day or other
we too grow old and die like beasts
return to the earth
vanish towards the sky
Yet the world unchanging
as we live on keeps prodding us awake
with an old old question
Only look!
Isn't this new and amazing and lovely?
Every year the deep perfume
of the lilac growing on a rubbish dump
filling the back-streets
An unsightly prickly cactus
dangling from the corner of a broken pot
blooming with one bright flower
after long restless nights
Springing from a pond's black slime
the bright form of a lotus flower
And surely
a child's sweet smile
sprung from a dark human womb
makes us still more perplexed?
We oblige our children
to wear shoes in case
they tread barefoot on the ground
and when their hands get muddy
we wipe them off saying That's dirty
For goodness sake!
Not rooted in the ground
their bodies not smeared with mud
the children's bursting hearts
their bouncing bodies
as they frolic and grow
all that welling energy
Where does it come from?

The depths of a clam

After they got married the girl never once confessed her first love affair. And of course her husband never got round to telling his secrets. In any case, as they went on living their lives were nothing but disenchantment. In order deliberately to conceal their disenchantment they said countless things, but there were still things they did not say.

The disenchantment built up like lead inside their bodies. The words they could not say hardened in their breasts like cancerous cells.

Although the disenchantment was unavoidable they always wanted to speak. They wanted to pour out their hearts to someone. It seemed that so long as nobody was going to remember they would be able to relax and tell it all at length.

At times it happened that other people said something similar. Or while reading they would discover a passage to that effect and thankfully underline it. Or they heard music that was more explicit than words. Yet to the very end their lips remained sealed like clams.

Finally, after living long years in unending disenchantment, still treasuring their secrets, they died. In so far as they were silent history was concealed and truth was hidden. And so today, as we repeat their life and discern those hidden depths, we still believe that this world is worth living in at least once.

Mount Inwang

Majestic Mount Inwang!
In old days a breeding-place of tigers
and for five hundred years rising
on the outskirts of the capital
then called Hanyang
gazing down on the joys and sorrows
of Seoul as if on childhood toys
The home of my remote grandfather
Where now is the trustworthy face
of that tremendous rocky slide
I used to itch to climb when I was a child?
In the pine groves of the steep valley
where pure water used to run between the rocks
today broken glass and plastic bags lie scattered
A grey oily haze shimmers
veiling the mountain mass
and now its mighty spurs
criss-crossed in all directions with asphalt roads
imprisoned in the midst of a population of 8 million
seem about to collapse
panting and gasping for breath
showing only a dessicated profile
a shabby back
slumped down on one edge of downtown Seoul
reduced in old age to life in a rented room
Poor Mount Inwang!

Water-melons

It was just the same last year
Every year at the bus-stop
in air thick with exhaust-fumes
a woman looking like Teresa
is selling papers while
beneath the elevated highway kids
dressed only in tee-shirt and shorts
are riding bikes
and at the fishy entry to the market
the strawberry-man has heaped
his pushcart with round water-melons
looking rather like the eggs a zebra might lay
At one end of an alley is a tavern where
widow and children have sat down together
and rapidly devoured a huge water-melon
then still sweating hungrily
begin to prepare dog stew
It was just the same this time last year
No new summer ever comes
by night the summer gets no deeper
unchanged the summer simply ends
So maybe having no home to return to
summer will always be like this
until melons grow square?

To the Korean bear

Is there anything new under the sun?
Creation too is nothing more than an effect
In the beginning there was a cause
followed by an effect
That effect in turn became a cause
and that cause once again gave birth to an effect
Old cause and effect were replaced
by new cause and effect
until at last they arrived at today
In which case yesterday is today's cause
and today is yesterday's effect
while today is tomorrow's cause
and tomorrow is undoubtedly today's effect
Foolish bear trying to separate cause and effect!
Don't try to manufacture a causeless effect
calling a new cause an old effect
and an old effect a new cause
Sometimes even death can become a cause
And there is nothing new under the sun

Old Marx

Look my young friend
That's not what history is like
it's not what you think it's like
it's not something that unfolds dialectically
and literature too is not like that
it's not what you think it's like
it's not something that changes logically
You are young
it's OK if you still don't know
but just suppose that the moment
you finally realize that really
history and literature are not like that
comes when you have already reached the age
where you can no longer change anything
in your life?
Look my young friend
Ideology in the head
can never become love in the heart
Even though our opinions may differ
how fortunate it is
that each one of us lives our share
and how unsatisfying
that each one of us lives only once
then is dead and gone
Even though we die and become the past
history remains as the present
and literature honestly records
the complexities of life in days gone by
Look my young friend
Take care
that your heart doesn't harden
before your body has had time to grow old
Take care!

Seaweed

The seashore is swept by a fresh tang
of brown seaweed
A fishing boat bringing back the sun
drops anchor and morning light spreads across the sand
having spent the night crossing oceans
Waves break softly
bringing their soft motion to an end while
with a little dog leading the way
women and children
go running along kicking up the water
As gulls wheel screaming
flapping sea-bream
and wriggling eels
with sea-slugs and shellfish
are still sunk deep
in their watery dreams
Let's not ask the price of fish
but gather up the seaweed
scattered across the shore for our share
and before the deep-sea pearl
can be sent to the distant city for sale
let's return
living fish to the fishermen
the breathing sea to the fish

The birth of a stone

In those deep mountain ravines
I wonder if there are stones
that no one has ever visited?
I went up the mountain
in quest of a stone no one had ever seen
from the remotest of times

Under ancient pines
on steep pathless slopes
there was a stone
I wonder
how long
this stone all thick with moss
has been
here?

Two thousand years? Two million? Two billion?
No
Not at all
If really till now no one
has ever seen this stone
it is only
here
from now on
This stone
was only born
the moment I first saw it

A missing person: ID number 15.08.45

Today is National Liberation Day, a Saturday and a holiday, the last long weekend of this particularly hot summer. We shall all fight to get out of the city and hurry to the seaside or up a mountain to spend a pleasant day.

When was that day? I've forgotten it and you.

Turning your back on the fiercely beating rays of the morning sun you set out on your long journey westwards. And a sturdy shadow like that of a giant was there before you guiding you on.

You walked briskly and ran panting.

On a midday crest you stood trampling your shadow and proudly wiped away the sweat. If only we could have stopped the flow of time there we would surely never have been parted.

On the slanting downhill path one two in a flash the leaves had fallen and the shadow dogging you had lost its strength too and drooped along burdening your footsteps.

Finally, when twilight on the snow-covered plains had soaked you through, your exhausted shadow abandoned you and you went on alone into the realms of night. You only came to a halt once enclosed in dazzling dark.

Then you would sit the whole day long idly without even a shadow, beside the tomb where the pigeons called and the magpies came down to preen their feathers.

Sometimes becoming a faded ghost you would visit me in bat-fluttering dreams.

That day you suddenly entered the courtyard of our house. Now become a tiny child, with a tiny shadow, wearing your familiar belt, smiling bright as the sun you appeared before me.

Who are you who went on ahead? Who are you who now follow along behind me? And when is today?

Two generations

In the old days
when even state officials wore uniforms
in the servants' quarters
in the outer compound
lived the Kangs husband and wife
The woman drew water
the man was yoked to a rickshaw
both worked for the master's house
but they cooked and ate apart

Today
when even school uniforms have disappeared
driver Kang and his wife
live in a nine-foot-long room
attached to the garage
The wife does the washing for the main house
but they cook and eat apart
and 'Mister' Kang is yoked to a Mercedes

Roadside trees in April

Their tops were cut off long ago
so as not to touch the power lines
This year even their limbs have been lopped
so they cannot sway if a spring breeze blows
and only the trunks remain like torsos
suffocating and grim
When the lilac perfume deepens
memories of another April day return
but now every trailing branch has been trimmed
so that the street-side weeping willows
lined up in rows
unable even to unfold new leaves
seething with impatience but
unable to utter even a cry
are putting out leaves from their trunks

Evening in May

Borne on the early summer breeze
gloomy news
Emerging from some house or other
clumsy piano sounds

Backhaus is already dead
now Rubinstein is getting old
but regardless of adults' despair
there are children beginning Bayer I

and because of this hope
that cannot be wrapped up
in newspaper and thrown away
darkness drops shamefaced
down every quiet street

A kind of confession

Perhaps I was a thoughtless kind of man? I mean I wanted to become a woman.

Not because I had to shave every day, or wear long pants even in summer and sweat, or defend the nation and earn money, not for that kind of reason.

But because I detested the role of a man, not allowed to love anybody, or detest anybody, and not just to keep quiet either, and if you don't win you lose.

But then when I really became a woman, I loved all the men of the world — students, stevedores, farmers, day-labourers, loafers, policemen, criminals, engineers, seamen, second-hand dealers, soldiers, politicians, tradesmen, brokers, and all, indiscriminately, and they called me a whore, while the women spat at me.

I only just escaped being dragged off to prison for not observing men's customs and women's proper place. A woman's role seemed even more difficult.

So then I wanted to become something that was neither man nor woman, that is to say not human.

So last spring I became a dog. Just as I was discovering how much faster you can go on four feet than on two, summer came.

People casually caught dogs, killed them with a blow and tossed them into seething pots. Many of my fellows lost their lives by sheer bad luck.

It was by no skill of mine that I managed to survive that long dreadful summer hidden without being able even to bark once. I am still alive, but I can never become a truly dog-like dog.

I wonder, might there somewhere be a land where they don't eat dog, a dogs' Paradise?

The garbage-collectors

You know nothing about us at all
Of course you think that
with the money we get from collecting garbage
we cover the cost of a drink on snowy days
and that with three years' savings
we buy a hand-cart and set ourselves up
as dealers in scrap and second-hand junk
but that's not the case
We are nothing at all like those
who pass giving a few cents' worth of pop-corn
in exchange for old magazines and newspapers
for discarded empty bottles and even scrap iron
those who stand guarding the alleys to the world beyond
with an eye on the corpses' gold teeth
We return burnt coal-briquettes to the soil
on the garbage-tips where dead money is thrown
the places where all the world's desires end up
Odd ownerless shoes and blood-stained rags
stinking fish-bones and strips of split plastic
all gathering together in a friendly way
scattering in the wind and soaking in the rain
set out homewards from the garbage-tip
We who here on earth's last precipice
burn up the stench of this sickening world
we are nothing like them at all
All you who can hear only an idle spring day's languor
in the clacking scissors of junk- and scrap-dealers
and run as far as you can from the garbage-tip
on your way to the bank
on your way to church
you know nothing about us at all

Kim with crutch

5 basement levels
30 floors above ground
150,000 square yards of floor space
When they were doing the groundwork
for Seoul Building
Kim did the rough jobs
Up and down the dizzying scaffolding
he carried loads of gravel
he helped with the plastering
he stuck on tiles
he fixed window-frames
Under Seoul Building's foundation stone
lie some 3 years of Kim's hard life
and somewhere up the dizzying emergency stairs
that go snaking heavenwards
is stuck
the left leg Kim lost there
Luckily he was wearing a safety helmet
so he escaped death by a hair's breadth
and six months later
when Kim came out of hospital on crutches
Seoul Building towering aloft
had become a well-known feature of the capital
Department stores with every kind of everything
a hotel too luxurious to sleep in
saunas and restaurants and financial company offices
everywhere white-clean men
busily banging away on computers
girls looking like screw-holes
noisily chewing gum
and recalling last night
with even time bought and sold for cash
it was a TV screen come alive

Wanting only to see how that spot
at the entrance to the emergency stairs

on the 13th floor
where he had tripped and gone headlong
had been finished off
Kim went hobbling along
to visit his former work-site
Suppose he happened to meet Lee the welder
then they might down a daytime glass
to celebrate
But at the entrance to Seoul Building
a janitor wearing a necktie
stopped him
saying people without work can't come in here
and at the back door where the garbage goes out
a fearsome guard blocked his path
so Kim turned away
Where did he go?

People I long to meet

They are all strangers to me
And yet the faces are strangely familiar
How many familiar strangers there are!
I wonder where we first met?
In the nursery-school garden
where a brood of chicks pecked at feed?
At the country market-place
where we bought and ate spun-candy?
On a bench in the school playground
newly blooming with acacia-flowers?
Was it sitting under a scorching sun
resisting on the roof of a sewing-factory?
Or being driven like animals
from springtime streets with streaming eyes?
Was it in the little night-guard's room
playing checkers to decide who paid for the drinks?
Or high up on a mountain
pantingly pursuing spies?
Was it in front of a prison at dawn
as we waited for friends?
In a room in an alley-way inn
with bean-curd sellers passing by outside?
Or in the corridor outside a maternity ward
chain-smoking as we waited?
Was it hawking loads of garlic
round apartment complexes?
Was it in a tax-office filing VAT returns?
Maybe in a suburban cinema
during a civil-defence training session?
Perhaps in some corner seat of a coffee-shop
discreetly handing over money in a white envelope?
Were we waiting to change planes
in some airport transit area?
Was it as we spent the night at a wake
in some house of mourning?
None of those

They are all lying memories
false illusions
We only brushed past each other
we never really met
They are all familiar-faced strangers
The strangers I know are so very few!

Trickery

Just five coins
If you toss them
the result is obvious
heads
or
tails

yet by deception
mixed
exchanged
tossed
picked up

even though you try all kinds of
permutations and combinations
you can do nothing about it
if you put down your money
in the time it takes to blink
the banker has grabbed it

Rub your eyes
and look again
still just five coins
heads
or
tails

nothing has changed
only the question
Who's grabbing the money?

Hope

And strictly speaking
the word hope
is surely a foreign word?
Talking about despair
with a friend who came
late one night
soaked with rain
I thought seriously about hope
He quoted Benjamin
saying that hope is something
for the despairing
apeing Descartes
with I despair
therefore I hope
But I wonder if what was said
by that Jew driven by despair
to end his life
was wrong?
Hope is decidedly not
for the despairing
since it is for those
who have not lost hope
In that case I wonder if we
discussing hope all night
like hunted Jews
are already despairing or
have not yet lost hope?
When curfew time ended
he disappeared into the dark
his bloodshot eyes bright with despair
Truly hope is always there ahead
even in hours of despair
not something that comes from somewhere else
not something somebody else gives us
but something we get by fighting
and have to defend
Hope
is certainly no
foreign word

I wonder who

I wonder who has abolished the downtown bus-stops

I wonder who is blowing a whistle far away
as he follows along behind us
eavesdropping on what we say
spying on our loves
he has gone off robbing us of our deep sleep
Our happy home has been raided like a brothel
our laboriously cultivated flowerbeds
trampled underfoot
I wonder who has dirtied our pure skies
put barbed-wire round our green villages
emptied waste oil into our broad oceans
disturbed our serious meetings
stopped our forceful steps
arrested our honest neighbours
I wonder who is pointing a gun at our backs
With our eyes blindfolded
our mouths gagged
throats strangling
veins pumped up
I wonder who has entered our heads
and is sticking a knife into our brains
reading things we never wrote
I wonder who is beating a drum far away
as he drives us up a blind alley

I wonder who is this someone we didn't invite.

Sketch of a fetish

He is no common man
definitely not an ordinary man
Far more lenient than a common man
far crueller than an ordinary man
he is not some meek kind of man
who endures hardship patiently
deliberately hiding his tears
He is not a man who gazes at the moon
longing for days gone by
Nimbly seizing the ball
like a goalkeeper before a tense crowd
he is not a man who works all day
and then goes home in the evening
He is not the kind of man who keeps to his lane
for fear of the traffic patrols
He is not a man who speaks in words
as he takes over all the best expressions
producing an urn of white silence
He is not someone who gazes
at the endlessly rolling waves
and fathoms the ocean's heart
He is not a man who hastens
onwards at dawn firm in the conviction
that yesterday's I is alone believable
He is not the kind of man who lowers his head
and silently follows after
Taking up sacred burdens beyond his power
and marching on and on
he is definitely not an ordinary man
not a common man
in short not a man at all

Opinions concerning the solar calendar

No matter what you say
a year of 365 days
is much too short
To go on doing the things you've begun
and complete the things you've been doing
no matter what you say
it's much too short
If I had power
if I had the power to control time
I'd at once arrange it so that from now on
the calendar would be corrected
and a New Year come only
once every three years

(Such were the thoughts of one person
celebrating New Year
while everybody else thought as follows)

No matter what you say
a year of 365 days
is much too long
To go on doing the things you've begun
and complete the things you've been doing
no matter what you say
it's much too long
If we had our way
if we had our way about how the globe turns
we'd at once unite our strength
and arrange it so that from now on
a New Year would come
three times a year
a new springtime would come
three times a year

Face and mirror

If you look into a bumpy mirror
down drop the eyes beneath the chin
up goes your nose above the eyes
an ear sprouts like a horn on top of your head
and your canines stick out like Dracula's
Do our faces really look like that?
Or is it all the mirror's fault?

If a Dracula with eyes beneath his chin
and a nose stuck on above his eyes
an ear sprouting like a horn on top of his head
and with canines sticking out
looks into a bumpy mirror
his appearance becomes that of a handsome fellow
Does Dracula's face really look like that?
Or is it all the mirror's fault?

It's really a trifling wish I know
but how I long to have a mirror
in which people look like people
and Dracula looks like Dracula

Forgotten friends

They too know the taste of fragrant coffee drunk after taking a bath on waking up late.

They too have spent happy Sundays in the Children's Park with pretty infants in tow.

They too recall the autumn seaside where we ate cold oysters and drank warm rice wine.

But nowadays many have gone to places you can't expect news from.

One friend stopped smoking for lack of spending-money, another out of spite only drank more.

Another went into business too rashly and lost even his rented house but they say that since last autumn he's been working in a house-agent's office down south of the river. It seems he has got much better at checkers but has a hard time making both ends meet.

There is also the friend who had a bitter experience: he cut off his hair and was going to enter a temple and become a monk, only he was arrested on suspicion of being a spy.

This one thanks to his wife's work as a teacher closetted himself at home and said he was going to translate Adorno. When I met him again after a long interval his stomach was sticking out like a fat frog's.

Cleaning shoes is hard of course, but they say that despite appearances setting up a street-side bar is just as hard unless you know the right people.

One friend opened a barber's shop and failed, sold monthly magazines but gave up, drove a taxi but had an accident, finally he was expressing an intention of becoming an undertaker, but succeeded in dying of hepatitis leaving one fourth-grade child.

The world has lost its mind and forgotten them all for far too long.

Only people who think of tetanus germs as soon as they see a drop of blood welling at the tip of a finger feel concerned about the future of Iran, on seeing pictures of the Ayatollah Khomeiny in the papers.

Tricolour flag

In the land of mists everybody
wanted to become a civil servant
then once they had become civil servants
they put on black uniforms
and prepared to wield power
In the end everyone had become a civil servant
and there were no citizens left
to pay taxes
They found themselves obliged
to take turns acting as citizens
just as they did night-duty and late shifts

In the land of mists everybody
wanted to become a shopkeeper
then once they had become shopkeepers
they put on yellow uniforms
and prepared to earn money
In the end everyone had become a shopkeeper
and there were no customers left
to buy things
They found themselves obliged
to elect customers
just as they chose chairmen for associations

In the land of mists everybody
wanted to become a soldier
then once they had become soldiers
they put on green uniforms
and prepared to defend the nation
In the end everyone had become a soldier
and there were no civilians left to defend
They found themselves obliged
to reduce the numbers under arms
and enter public service as civilians
just as they went on night-watch or guard-duty

(It has only recently been discovered that this has some
connection with the black, yellow and green tricolour flag
of the land of mists)

Winter 1981

A flood of water
exploded suddenly spouting
in mine galleries
300 yards underground
where day and night blend
in a single black sweat
breathlessly pouring
Black death
the spurting liquid coal
filled the shafts in a flash
but some fought against
the chill mine-water
for one day two days three
barely surviving
in emergency shafts then
time flowed again
life was reborn

That event rubbing out lives
like scribbles
our lives of weary pain
crimson lives that cannot
for one minute rest
was certainly no mechanical error
Nor was it an error
on the part of those feeding data
into the computer
or an error of the one
who gave them instructions
The orders he received
came from a distant place
Too far away
for us to see where it lies
that place lies in our head
in our breast
and in our heart as well

If we close our eyes
and listen hard to
the sound of the wind
crossing steep mountains
and passing through rusty fences
to reach us
stripped of flesh and blood
whistling words wandering
come clawing at the air
and sting the tongue
In every street slogans of silence
lie scattered like corpses
and on every store bargain-sale signs
flap like so many funeral banners
but tell me where now is our mother tongue
that calls freedom freedom
that calls love love?

Evening comes and the whistle
we have heard all day falls silent
the glassed-in shop fronts
are all closed
We didn't sleep
but lay awake
and counting the heart-beats
we thought of names
for the baby soon to be born
Once again when day dawns
we shall put on yesterday's clothes
but now we will not run on command
We'll go walking slowly
along early morning misty roads
bringing forgotten words back to life
and accept
even the cancer cells
spreading within our bodies
as part of life

To my children

Never go into dangerous places
and it is better to do nothing
that might make you suspect
That's what my deceased father
always used to say
Obedient to his words
I stayed indoors
like a cat on a sunny back porch
I was always a sweet child
Someone who lives peacefully
someone who never does anything
someone who leaves no trace behind
according to his words if you live like that
what difficulties can you have in life?
I was willing but it is not so easy
to live like that either
Maybe because I lack mental stamina?
On days typhoons blow
sitting indoors at home
sorting out dogeared books
and burning old diaries
I keep tearing things up
so that nothing will remain
For suppose something were to remain!
And even if one day suddenly
I became unable to do this
suppose somebody were to remember me!
But in any case maybe a strange
telephone call will come first
When an earthquake strikes
just staying indoors is dangerous too
Even doing nothing
makes you suspect
Having shunned the sin of
the quiet life
this is what I will tell my children
Don't live peacefully
At least do something
No matter how shameful the trace
leave something behind

No! Not so

All the pain of the leaves
as they burst in anguish
through their hardened shells
and that of azaleas in flower
had become a furious cry
on that day the earth shook
as he raced ahead of the others
then fell near the Blue House
His bag still bulging
with lunchbox and dictionary
he fell to the roadway
never to rise again
robbed of his bright smile
and supple movements
So did he die in vain
in the twentieth year of his youth?

No
Not at all
Since the day he cried Drive them out
he has become a lion eternally young
roaring fiercely
on the central campus lawn
he has become a fountain
that rises skywards
His surviving companions sheepishly
graduated and did their military service
got married and had children so that
before you knew it today they are
middle-aged wage-earners
while he has remained unchanging
a young university student
attending lectures regularly
absorbed in impassioned debates
skillfully pursuing the ball
Look there and see his vital image

unswervingly following truth
in his proud successor
our promising son
defending the nation with his whole being
tending anew the ideals
we had forgotten

So it is
Since the day he fell near the Blue House
endlessly rising again
he races on
ahead of us

Autumn 1983–
Spring 1986

Tightropes

There's no audience and yet
everyone's carrying a pole
and walking the tightrope high in the air
where so many ropes are criss-crossed
that if there's no way ahead on one
they jump across to the next
and even when resting keep switching
seats from one to another and back
but if you fall
between the ropes you
vanish
into the unfathomed dark
With so many ropes criss-crossing
it sometimes looks like solid ground
but if you blink one eye and
make a false step
you've had it so
trying hard not to fall
controlling their swaying bodies
everyone's ever so cautiously
toeing the line

One finger

Eyes meeting by chance
trembled for a moment like compass needles
A space once open was now shut
filled up tightly
endlessly deeply yet
when we overlapped
by a single finger's length
the whole world pierced
and passed burning through
Somewhere in the world gone by
once for a moment in time now lost
as dull eyes stood riveted
throats tighting
a moment passed
endlessly distant yet
with only the width of one finger between
unsure if they touched the ground or not
two pairs of feet trailed indifferently

Pagoda tree

The local people used to call that tree where every night the owl came and shrieked a pagoda tree.

The pagoda tree cast a broad shadow by the well-side. The bucket vanished, a pump appeared, later they introduced a piped water supply, and in that place a short while ago a filling station arose, but still the pagoda tree stands there unchanged.

During the Korean War, the bombed-out wreck of an army truck lay for a long time abandoned beneath the pagoda tree. After any items fit for the scrap dealers had been torn away, it became a plaything for the children and for almost 3 years that great lump of iron lay there rusting red until at last it broke up and disappeared.

A few scraps of shrapnel stuck into the pagoda tree too, but those bits of metal gradually rusted and were absorbed by the sap, a gnarl appeared over the spot. At some time or other a nature protection sign has been hung there.

When I look at that pagoda tree, still now I long to stroke its great bulk, to lean against it, go climbing up into it, even to become its roots or branches. And whether I'm hurrying along on foot, or in a taxi, whenever I pass before it a feeling of shame arises.

For I keep thinking that motion is what that pagoda tree is doing, while standing fixed in one spot today as of old is what in reality I myself am doing.

Before an old incense burner

Were those days really different from now?
Everyone is ready to admire a well-turned, well-shaped,
pretty incense burner
and treasure it lovingly
but this is no exquisitely beautiful
lidded incense burner in inlaid celadon
giving a glimpse of the clouds and lotus flowers
of 800 years ago
It is one that came cracked and twisted from the kiln
incense was never once burned in it
it just lay kicking around in some potter's shed
and precisely this one ugly squarish pot
that endured all that time
and has survived until today
within its battered form
holds all the skies of ancient Koryo

Autumn sky

Not a single cloud
and the blue autumn sky
looms empty
Nothing covering the earth
nothing veiling the sky
sunlight pouring down
the wind blowing

My heart is on edge
Suppose a dead leaf should fall
across the sky?

I wonder how long
it can endure?
As if on a word of command
everything has been swept clean away
and without a single cloud
the blue autumn sky
looms fearful

April–May

I'm not sure when it began
but every year now April only comes
and doesn't go
Azaleas and forsythias bloom everywhere
and as the scent of lilac strengthens
the torn and faded banner flaps again
and the old wound in my side throbs
all my bruised bones ache separately
and from the dry black wound
blood flows again
Relapse or resurrection I wonder?
The acacias bloom gloriously
and one day sad with the cuckoo's call
along the banks between green sprouting rice-fields
women pass bearing a coffin
while from rubbish dumps in woods or at roadsides
bodies denied even a shroud rise up
unsleeping
unrotting
unforgotten
Time only thickens
I'm not sure when it began
but every year now May only comes
and doesn't go

The summer there were no cicadas

One cicada was singing in a persimmon tree
then flew off but was abruptly checked in mid-air
Ahah a spider's web spreading wide!
The spider hiding under the edge of the roof
had the struggling cicada tied up in a flash
no point in mentioning anything like
conscience or ideas
no place for regret or excuses
At the end of seven years' preparation
the cicada's lovely voice
after scarcely seven days ended up
as a spider's supper
If you're caught like that you've had it
The cicadas stopped singing
and flying
It was a remarkably long hot summer

A Song of Books

Revolution's a dangerous thing
a forbidden game
but only consider history
has there ever been a single instance
where a great nation
or a new age
has come to birth
without a terrible revolution?

If something containing
a wonderful idea
in a new language
is what is called a great book
it is the power of the mind
the dream in the heart
that will lead history forward

But the people who launch revolutions
are always those who most fear revolutions
and their natural disposition being to dislike books
instead of reading great books
they reflect on which books to ban

Now the people who ban books
are really banning thought and feeling
'the people who burn books
are really burning people'
and as a result they bring themselves down
Just think back through history
surely book-banning and book-burning
are even more dangerous games than revolutions!

To the Chairman of the Board

Your chest covered with decorations you
smoked a cigarette as you brooded on the past
'That was no fault of mine
On the battlefield you are either friend or foe'
If only you had smoked another pipe
before you gave the orders
wouldn't today have been a little different?

Don't you still consider
every person in this world
either an enemy or a friend
as you go off horse-riding every morning
with a round of golf at weekends
now you are an honourably retired general?

In that case is Mister Kim from the housing agency
friend or enemy?
And section-head Lee who now drives his own car
Miss Park there waiting for the elevator
or all those students crowded in the library
are they friend or enemy?
And Mr Chong from the co-operative market
engineer Choe from the production department
or those youngsters with their suspicious activities
are they enemy or friend?
And what of all those people
crowding the streets the stations the shops
and you yourself now become President of the Board
for heaven's sake
enemy or friend?

The new door

So that one single person
can go in and out about once a year
they have set up this enormous doorway
slap in the middle
with a dozen men guarding it day and night
'Keep out'
Only look at that tremendous doorway
that ordinary people
may not use
gaping wide open for just one man
to go in by
and always closed
to everyone else

That's not made to be opened
it's made to be shut
that's not made to be gone through
it's made to be blocked
that's not a door for us
it's a wall
so let's smash down
that wall
blocking our way

Let's destroy
those marble stairs
no one is permitted to tread on
let's uproot
those granite pillars
nobody is allowed to approach
let's break down
that iron gate
none can enter and leave by

Yes let's destroy them
and after destroying that great door
no one can use
instead let's build
a wall
and in that wall
let's build a new door
let's build a door
everyone can
go in and out by

Mr O's job

I often wondered what could be the job
of our neighbour Mr O

It's just that in front of his house
there was an unusually bright street light
he kept no clear working hours
and since you never met him in the road
there was no way of knowing his position
but then one day down at the corner a sign appeared
indicating someone in Mr O's house had died
and at once black official cars began driving up
filling the narrow roadway and for several days
a succession of expensive cars
each bearing a single needle-eyed passenger
kept arriving
and then soon leaving again
but there was no one came by taxi
or on foot to offer condolence

So now at last I know
what Mr O's job is

Wisdom tooth

It's a nuisance
it ought to come out
it will just go rotten
and damage the molars
a wisdom tooth should come out
I don't know why they grow at all
you can't chew with them
(a doctor's words are always
medically correct)
But will taking it out
really be the cure?
(Frightened patients
are invariably pig-headed)
But I don't think I will get rid
of this wretched tooth
though its aching keeps me awake at night
it may be a bothersome wisdom tooth
but who if not I will chew
and be capable of patiently enduring
and treasuring
this part of myself
that gives me my share of pain?

Young people like trees

Even in midwinter
if we have a few days of mild weather
the careless forsythia peeks out yellow cheeks
When spring comes
everywhere azaleas burst into flower
heedless of late frosts
but will anyone say
a blossoming flower's heart is fragile
and repress it?
Can any say
that the power of the roots
plunging deep into the dark ground is invisible
and despise it?
So with your roots plunged deep in the ground
and bearing dreams blossoming skywards
at the tips of your highest branches
may you young people like trees
springing up vigorously
pushing down quietly
spread bright and wide
but do not by some chance forget
that even when from the topmost tip of a lofty branch
can be glimpsed the far side of the plains
unless the roots remain fixed in the ground
and spring water turned into sap
flows secretly inside the trunk
neither the acacia nor the lilac
whose perfume drifts from afar on the wind
would ever be able to bloom

People on the bus

Fumes of tear-gas rise
from young people carrying books
When they pass through university areas
the people on the bus
wipe their eyes
and sneeze
and though their noses run
they say nothing
They too used to go to school
now they have done military service
they pay their taxes
raise their families
they are ordinary citizens
struggling through life
those things the young dislike
they are none too fond of either
but they are just grown-ups with dirty hands
unable to have a natural opinion
about square-shaped things
So those who get on the bus
amidst shouted slogans
and hurtling stones
dodging volleys of tear-gas bombs
their mouths still covered with handkerchiefs
they are no mere idle on-lookers
they are not unconcerned passers-by
Their names are unknown but
who are these oh so familiar people?

To a young man driving his own car

So you're already driving your own car
I'll bet your friends are jealous
As you were learning to drive
I thought how splendid for you
to go speeding everywhere
Getting any kind of licence is good
I often said
Now you speed about in your car
you can't see the roadside trees changing
with the seasons
you can't see the merchants selling fruit
or fish at the roadside
you can't see the woman running along
with a sick child slung on her back
Always on the look-out for traffic-patrols
and red lights
your eyes fixed straight ahead
you speed about
your eyes have grown sharper
your mind has grown busier
and though the price of fuel
may go up even more
and exhaust fumes block your view
you drive around
and do not intend to walk anywhere I'm sure
and those years of youth that people spend
walking or running
getting about by bus or subway
you are spending at over 40 mph
When I see you speeding along in your car
I feel you have isolated yourself
too lightly
and my heart grows heavy

Going up over Buk-han hill

If you go up the road over Buk-han hill
in valleys thick with trees and bushes
where the mountain-birds sing sweetly
elegant mansions multiply
so it's rather like walking
through the pictures in a calendar
Most of these houses
with their huge watch-dogs
have no name-plate at the door
and are always quite empty
Maybe their owners spend the whole day
earning money out on the market-place
shedding their blood on the battle-field
defending their own money and strength
they seem to have no time to come home
What a waste these big empty houses
Of course the people who work at home
never have this kind of house
What you call a house may be small
but it must have a roof to keep out rain and snow
and walls that are wind-proof
yet the people who actually live in houses
have nothing that really keeps out the weather
but when the roof leaks in the rainy season
they arrange buckets here and there on the floor
and get through the summer
When the wind comes in through cracks in the wall
they put on more clothes
and get through the winter
fighting the fumes from the coal-briquettes
Even without any garden or gateway
messy smelly shacks
bring life to bustling alleys
If you go up the road over Buk-han hill
with its wide asphalt surface
gloomy mansions multiply
where nobody is admiring the beautiful view
nobody breathing the fresh breeze
nobody listening to the sound of birds and streams
so it's like passing through the Village of Death

In those days

Was there anyone who didn't know?
What everyone felt
What everyone went through
Was there anyone who didn't know?

In those days
everybody knew
but pretended not to know
What no one could say
what no one could write
was spoken
in our language
written in our alphabet
and communicated

Was there anyone who didn't know?
Do not speak too glibly now times have changed
Stop and think
In those days
what did you do?

Springtime road

Once every month I went
following behind my father
on our way to pay our respects
at the tomb of my Stonewell Village grandma

Walking flip-flop
in white rubber shoes
along that four-mile path
with the dusty dried mud flying up
in the springtime drought
about the time we were treading on our shadows
we would arrive at Bellows Valley

Sprawled on the floor at the pedlar's inn
resting our legs a moment
while the oxcarts rumbled past
father would sip makkoli
and I would drink rice syrup

That spot where roadside larks
whirred skimming our heads
singing a weary drowziness
like heat-haze shimmering

Al these memories
come rushing back in vain
as today with the whole family
we go speeding in our car
along an asphalted road

Bones

When I saw on an X-ray film
the bones that hold up my body
they seemed not at all to be mine
The fractured rib was not
made of stainless steel
or of plastic
but neither was it the rafters
of a God-given soul

Dust of anchovies and eels
piling up over a few dozen years
hardening and growing into bones
that I have never once seen
and have taken too much for granted
Everything made of dust
gathered together and hardened
sometime or other cracks breaks
and is finally smashed back into dust

The bones that hold up my body too
will turn at last to dust
and after drifting like snow-flakes through space
will one day pile up again
My fractured rib too
sometime or other will twirl
here and there as dust no longer mine
and be quite unable to remember anything of my pain

These bones will break and leave me
In the bustling market and streets too
no one stays very long
all hurry past and vanish
and between the gaunt but lingering trees
the wind comes blowing
It too belongs to no one

Electrocardiogram

Borne on the autumn breeze
the dragonflies go soaring high
Though the leaves fall
the resident birds have nowhere to go
and their songs become bitter
The frosts come
and the days end early
Just as the first snowflakes come fluttering
the calls of the passing migrant birds fall silent
and the winter hills become deep midnight
dark and sombre
The earth falls fast asleep
and though the sun appears it does not wake

When the busy chatter of the birds
charms the flowers to bloom again
and every time the turtledoves coo
the village grows a little brighter
when the cuckoo and the warbler call
the mountains grow radiant
and when it becomes high summer
with the songs of cicadas and insects
pouring out like streams
to the strong pulse of the trees
the earth too throbs
and in my flickering memory
the butterfly I saw yesterday comes fluttering by

Familiar shoes

A pair of shoes are lying
today in front of the door of 1301
The heels are worn down slantwise
the toes scuffed pale
those old shoes are undoubtedly
the ones he wore
Who knows perhaps when he was young
he slaved in the fields
to bring up his family
After losing his old wife
he was obliged to leave his village
and finally ended up in his son's home
So he came to live silently
secluded like a criminal in a room
in New Town's high-rise apartment blocks
His grandchildren said he smelt and disliked him
his daughter-in-law found doing his washing a bind
his son was busy so they never met
Every night he watched the tele through to the end
Each morning going up the nearby hill
he would count the notes in his wallet
and examine his Farmers' Cooperative book
During the day he would stare down
from the veranda on the 13th floor
like a skinny animal trapped in a cage
If he encountered anyone in the elevator
he would quickly turn his gaze aside
and say nothing
He must have lived here about ten months
and we never once exchanged a greeting
but today his familiar shoes
are lying outside the door of 1301

A good son

One old friend of mine
lived with his widowed mother
until he had passed middle age
now his hair is greying

Today he is out shopping with his wife
He has a mourning badge for his mother
fixed to his lapel and together
they are choosing a tie

Since those two got married
I have never seen them look so carefree
and so cheerful!

An old pine tree

Old pine tree
under a preservation order
in the garden in front of the Saemaul Centre
you have been standing there unchanged
for a good hundred years now
casting your cool shade
and showing the movement of the breeze
Judging by your trunk where even the resin has dried up
your roots must have got diseased
but the people here
having no idea of how weary you feel
have enclosed your lower trunk in cement
and even given you injections
telling you to keep on standing there
It may not be at all desirable
but nothing is more natural than old age
and how you must wish after such a long time
just once to flop down and take a rest
Of course, several centuries may pass
before you rise again after resting
but who can dispel your drowsiness?
Well look at that! Finally closing your green eyes
after keeping them open for a century or more
you have fallen asleep standing up
old pine tree
with your drooping red branches

He

He is old and white-haired
like some distant forbear
and if you want to meet him
of course money or influence
are no help at all
In a cosy room with central heating
sitting in a comfy armchair praying
and singing with a gentle voice
you will never get beside him
For he is in a place no car
no matter how powerful can reach

If you really want to meet him
there is no other way than to walk there naked
the only way lies over stony fields and muddy tracks
that have never once been surfaced
walking sweating on your own two feet
If your feet get blistered collapse by the roadside
then hobble on up over the crest of the hill
and with a glance at the evening drawing in
scoop water thirstily from the stream and drink
then continue on along the dark night road
step after heavy step with never a milestone
and if you fall crawl groping on
That is what you must do

And if you reach his side in this way
there your knowledge and wealth will be useless
prayers or songs unnecessary
and instead of joy at finally meeting him
still now knowing who he is
dropping down beside him
you will fall into an endless sleep
from which there will be no rising

Mountain heart

On days when my heart grows grim
since I cannot be born again
I leave my quiet house
and go away to the mountains
If I climb to the top of Kunak Mountain
leaving the world to its own devices
as a wild cat slinks between
the scattered rocks and dense foliage
between the leaves of the dark-hooded oaks
and a lizard basking in the sunlight
on a rotting tree stump
I feel jealous of all these trees and beasts
that have the earth and the sky for their home
living at ease with just their bare bodies
and of those flowers and insects
that die and are reborn year by year
I let loose a heroic 'Yahoo'
but since there is no Lord of the mountain
all I get back is a wayfaring voice
I may climb the lofty peaks
or go down into the deep ravines
the mountain has no central point
only everywhere the chirping of mountain birds
mingles and flows with the foaming torrents
while the scent of the dark green forest
unfolds and rises cool
Unable to settle gently on a branch
unable to sleep huddled in a rocky crevice
unable to rot away with the dead leaves
leaving behind my heart
that longs to live in the mountains
I depart and
on the day I return from Kunak Mountain
now a nameless little hill
I am reborn
in house and village